Looking at Stars

Planets

Robin Kerrod

Belitha Press

First published in the UK in 2001 by
Belitha Press Limited, London House,
    Great Eastern Wharf, Parkgate Road,
    London SW11 4NQ

Copyright © Belitha Press Limited 2001
Text by Robin Kerrod

All rights reserved. No part of this book may be reproduced
or utilized in any form or by any means, electronic or
mechanical, including photocopying, recording or by any
information storage and retrieval system, without permission
in writing from the publisher, except by a reviewer who may
quote brief passages in a review.

ISBN 1 84138 331 7

British Library Cataloguing in Publication Data
for this book is available from the British Library.

Printed in Hong Kong

10 9 8 7 6 5 4 3 2 1

Editor: Veronica Ross
Designer: Helen James
Illustrator: Chris Forsey
Consultant: Doug Millard
Picture researcher: Diana Morris

Photo credits
E. Karkoschka (University of Arizona) & NASA/Spacecharts: 22b.
NASA: 29cl.
NASA/Spacecharts: front cover c, 1, 3, 4-5, 10bl, 10br, 11t, 12cl,
13b, 15tl, 15bl, 15r, 16t, 17tr, 18b, 18-19t, 19bl, 19br, 21t, 23tr, 24b, 24-5, 27tr.
Spacecharts: 11b, 12b, 16b, 17bl, 17br, 20bl, 20tr, 23tl, 25tr, 26bl,
27cl, 27bl, 28t, 29tr, 29cr, 30b.
Torleif Svensson/Stockmarket/Corbis: 13t.

Contents

Introducing the planets

On many nights of the year, some very bright stars appear in the sky. And, month by month, they slowly wander among the other stars. Ancient astronomers called these bright wandering stars **planets**.

But, the wandering stars are not stars at all. Stars are huge hot balls that give off light. The wandering stars – the planets – are very much smaller and colder. And they give off no light of their own. We see them only because they reflect light from the Sun towards us.

Moving in circles

The planets travel through space with the Sun. They are part of the Sun's family, or **Solar System**. With our eyes and through telescopes, we can see eight planets in the night sky. There is one more planet, which we know very well – the Earth.

Mars
228 000 000 km

Venus
108 000 000 km

Sun

Mercury
58 000 000 km

Earth
150 000 000 km

△ Inner planets
The four inner planets are Mercury, Venus, Earth and Mars. The figures give average distances from the Sun.

asteroids

Jupiter
778 000 000 km

Saturn
1 430 000 000 km

Round and round

All the planets circle the Sun. The Earth is one of four planets that circle quite close to the Sun, in the inner part of the Solar System. The others are Mercury, Venus and Mars. After Mars, there is a huge gap before the next planet, Jupiter. In this gap there are thousands of mini-planets, called the **asteroids**.

The planets further out are very far apart. Saturn is twice as far from the Sun as Jupiter, and Uranus is twice as far away as Saturn. The final two planets, Neptune and Pluto are too far away to be seen with our eyes. The further a planet is away from the Sun, the longer it takes to circle the Sun. Mercury takes only 88 days to circle the Sun. Pluto takes nearly 250 years.

▽ **Outer planets**

The five outer planets are Jupiter, Saturn, Uranus, Neptune and Pluto. The figures give average distances from the Sun.

Pluto
5 900 000 000 km

Uranus
2 870 000 000 km

Neptune
4 500 000 000 km

7

Little and large

To us, the Earth we live on seems huge. But it is one of the smallest of the planets. Earth's neighbours among the planets – Mercury, Venus and Mars – are even smaller. If you look at the picture, you can see how tiny they are compared with Jupiter, Saturn, Uranus and Neptune. These four planets are called the giant planets.

Earth and its three neighbours are all solid, rocky bodies, quite different from the giant planets, which are made up mainly of light gas. We often call them the **gas giants**. Tiny Pluto is in a class by itself. It is made up of a mixture of rock and ice.

Jupiter
142 200 km

Mercury
4874 km

Venus
12 104 km

Earth
12 756 km

Mars
6794 km

▷ *The nine planets differ greatly in size, from the very small (Pluto) to the very large (Jupiter). The figures give the diameter of each planet.*

Uranus
51 200 km

Saturn
120 000 km

Neptune
49 500 km

Pluto
2284 km

Scorching worlds

Mercury is the planet that is closest to the Sun. It is a small planet, not much bigger than our Moon. And, like the Moon, it is covered in huge **craters**. Mercury is so close to the Sun it gets very hot.

In places, temperatures rise to 430°C, which is nearly twice as hot as a kitchen oven. Mercury is a difficult planet to spot. It stays close to the Sun in the sky and is usually lost in the Sun's glare.

◁ **Like the Moon**
Craters cover almost all of Mercury, making it look much like the Moon.

▽ **In close-up**
The largest crater here is nearly 150 km across.

Evening star

Venus is an easier planet to find. On many nights it can be seen shining brightly in the west just after sunset. We call it the evening star. Venus is nearly as big as the Earth, and it comes closer to us than any other planet. But it is quite different from the Earth. It has a much thicker **atmosphere** (layer of gases). If you went to Venus, the atmosphere would crush you to death. The thick atmosphere also traps the Sun's heat, making the planet even hotter than Mercury.

△ **Cloudy weather**

Swirling clouds show up in Venus's thick and deadly atmosphere.

▽ **Volcanic activity**

Volcanoes *all over Venus have covered the planet with lava flows.*

Planet Earth

The Earth is home for millions of kinds of living things, from tiny plants to huge animals like whales. There are three reasons why things can live on Earth. It is not too hot and not too cold. It has water on the surface and oxygen in the atmosphere. All living things need warmth, water and oxygen.

△ Spaceship Earth
From space, the Earth looks beautiful. White clouds swirl above the blue seas.

▷ Fiery fountains
Fountains of molten lava from an erupting volcano. This shows that Earth is still a very active planet.

Rocky surface

The Earth is made up mainly of rock. But only about a third of the Earth's surface is rocky. This forms the land areas, or continents. The rest of the surface is covered with water, forming the oceans.

On the move

The continents do not stay in the same place all the time. They slowly move around. They sit on rocky islands, which float on a layer of hot, liquid rock. The Earth is not rocky all the way through. In the middle there is a big ball of iron. This turns the Earth into a kind of magnet.

△ **Life-giver**
Animals drink at a water-hole on the plains of East Africa. Life on Earth depends on water.

▷ **Drifting continents**
A view from space of Africa (left) and Arabia (right). The two land masses are slowly splitting apart.

Next-door neighbour

The **Moon** lights up the sky on most nights of the year. It is Earth's closest companion in space, only about 384,000 kilometres away. The Moon is Earth's only natural satellite.

It circles the Earth once a month. During this time, it seems to change shape, becoming bigger or smaller. We call these changes the **phases of the Moon.**

Sea of Cold

Sea of Showers

Sea of Serenity

Sea of Vapours

Ocean of Storms

Sea of Tranquillity

Sea of Crises

Sea of Fertility

Sea of Clouds

Sea of Nectar

◁ Dusty seas
The dark areas we see on the Moon are great plains. We call them seas.

▷ Moon-man
An Apollo astronaut exploring the Moon in 1972.

◁ **Moon rock**
The Moon is a rocky body, made up of volcanic rocks like this.

Dead world

The Moon is quite small, only 3476 kilometres across. This is about the same size across as the United States. It does not have any air, atmosphere, or water. Nothing can live on the Moon. It is a dead world.

Like all bodies in space the Moon has **gravity**, or a pull. And this pull affects the Earth. It tugs at the water of the oceans and makes the tides rise.

△ **Craters galore**
Craters large and small pepper the Moon's surface.

Red planet

Mars is quite an easy planet to spot in the night sky. It is often bright and has a reddish glow. That is why we call it the Red planet. Mars is a small world, only about half the size across as the Earth.

Mars is much colder than Earth. Frost often covers the ground. And there are caps (layers) of ice at Mars's north and south poles.

△ Clouds
Clouds cling to the slopes of Mars's biggest volcano, Olympus Mons. It is 25 km high.

▷ Ice
Ice covers Mars's north pole.

Ancient rivers

Today there is no liquid water on Mars. But many years ago there were probably rivers and even seas. Mars has many interesting features. It has vast sandy deserts and areas covered with craters. It has towering **volcanoes** and mazes of valleys. The biggest valley is Mariner Valley, which is nearly 5000 kilometres long. It is much longer, deeper and wider than the famous Grand Canyon in the United States.

▷ Frost

Frost gathers in a huge basin (top) in this view of a crescent Mars. And clouds cling to Olympus Mons volcano (bottom).

▽ Rocks

Small rocks are scattered all over Mars's surface. They contain a lot of iron, which makes them a reddish colour.

King planet

Ancient people named the planet Jupiter after the king of their gods. It is a good name because Jupiter is a king among the planets. It is bigger than all the other planets put together, and could swallow more than 1000 Earths.

Jupiter shines a brilliant white on many nights of the year. One reason why it shines so bright is that it has a thick, cloudy atmosphere, which reflects sunlight well.

△ **Voyager's view**

The Voyager 2 space probe's view of Jupiter, showing the Great Red Spot (bottom left) and the moon Io.

◁ **Big storm**

A close look at the Great Red Spot. It is an enormous swirling storm that has been raging for centuries.

Colourful atmosphere

In telescopes, Jupiter's atmosphere looks very colourful. It is crossed by pale and dark bands of orange and brown. These bands are clouds rushing round the planet at high speed. In and between the bands, there are great swirls and waves and coloured spots. These are very stormy regions. The biggest storm is a region called the Great Red Spot.

Underneath the atmosphere, Jupiter is completely covered by an ocean. It is not an ocean of water but an ocean of **liquid gas** (hydrogen).

▽ Great balls of fire
In 1994, over 20 bits of a comet (below) hit Jupiter. They caused great fireballs in the atmosphere (left).

Many moons

The Earth has one moon circling round it. But Jupiter has at least 16 moons. We can see the four biggest in binoculars. They are Io, Europa, Ganymede and Callisto.

Ganymede is the largest moon in the Solar System. It is bigger than the planet Mercury. Callisto is slightly smaller, but still bigger than Mercury. Io is about the same size as our Moon, while Europa is slightly smaller.

△ Ganymede
Diameter 5276 km

◁ Io
Diameter 3632 km

Rock and ice

Ganymede, Callisto and Europa are made up of rock and ice. Ganymede has a dark surface with many white spots. These spots show where **meteorites** have hit the surface and thrown out fresh white ice. Callisto is darker and has many more craters. Europa is pale and very smooth. It is covered with cracked ice.

△ Callisto
Diameter 4820 km

Rivers of sulphur

Io is completely different. It is vividly coloured yellow and orange. And in places volcanoes are erupting. They don't pour out liquid rock, but rivers of yellow sulphur.

△ Io's eruptions
Volcanoes erupt on Io. Molten sulphur pours onto the surface. Sulphur fumes spurt into the sky.

Ringed planet

Saturn is the second biggest planet, just smaller than Jupiter. But it never shines very brightly in the night sky because it is so far away – twice as far as Jupiter. In a telescope, Saturn looks different from all the other planets. This is because it has **rings** circling it. Saturn is similar to Jupiter. It is a gas giant, with bands of clouds in its atmosphere. Underneath the atmosphere there is a vast ocean of liquid gas.

◁ Stormy weather
Bands of clouds and storms show up in Saturn's atmosphere.

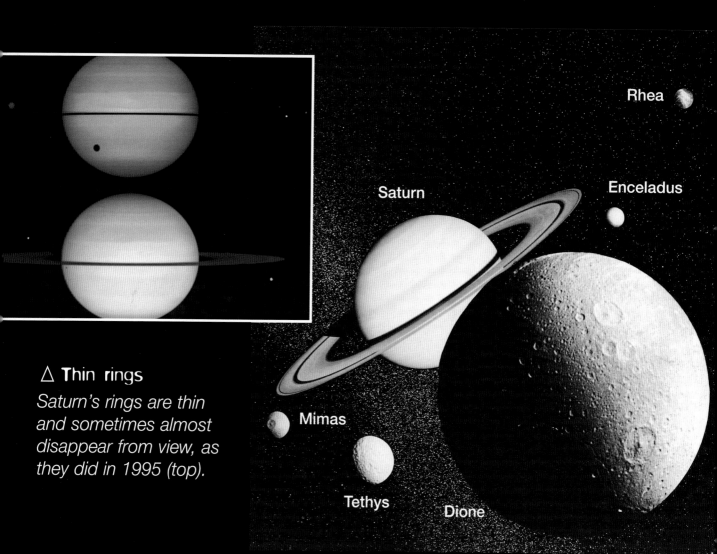

Rhea

Saturn

Enceladus

Mimas

Tethys

Dione

△ Thin rings

Saturn's rings are thin and sometimes almost disappear from view, as they did in 1995 (top).

△ Cratered moons

Saturn and five of its larger moons. Like the other moons, Dione is pitted with craters.

Many Moons

Like Jupiter, Saturn has many moons circling it – at least 18. The largest ones seem to be made up of rock and ice.

Biggest of all is Titan, about 5140 kilometres across.

Titan is the second largest moon in the Solar System. It is unusual because it has a thick atmosphere. Astronomers think that on Titan it may rain and snow liquid and frozen gas.

Rings of ice

▷ Ringside
What the rings would look like close-up.

Saturn has three main rings, which we can see from Earth. It also has several narrow faint rings that we can't see. All these rings are made up of millions upon millions of bits of ice, whizzing round at high speed. Some lumps are as big as boulders, others as small as pebbles.

△ Ringlets
Thousands of ringlets form the rings.

△ **Different particles**

This picture shows up differences between the particles that make up the ringlets.

Mysterious rings

Space probes have taken close-up pictures of Saturn's rings. The three rings we see from Earth are actually made up of thousands of ringlets. We don't know where the rings came from. They may be the remains of a moon, torn to pieces by Saturn's powerful gravity, or pull.

Distant twins

For centuries, people thought that Saturn was the most distant planet. But in 1781 an English astronomer named William Herschel discovered another one, twice as far away as Saturn. It was called Uranus.

In 1846 astronomers found a second new planet, twice as far away as Uranus. They called it Neptune. Astronomers realized that the Solar System was much bigger than they had thought.

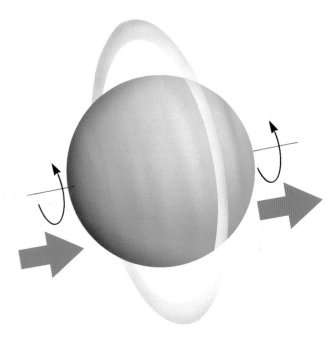

△ **Topsy-turvy**
Uranus spins on its side as it circles in orbit around the Sun.

◁ **Rings round Uranus**
Uranus has 11 faint rings circling round it.

▷ **Amazing Miranda**
Uranus's moon Miranda has the strangest markings on its surface.

▷ Neptune's atmosphere

Flecks of clouds and dark spots appear in Neptune's atmosphere. The big dark spot is a stormy region.

▽ Triton's geysers

Dark fumes erupt from geysers on Neptune's largest moon, Triton.

Vast oceans

Uranus and Neptune are nearly identical in size – about four times bigger across than the Earth. They both have a deep atmosphere and, underneath, an ocean containing water and liquid gases. They are both bluish in colour.

Uranus has more than 20 moons. It also has some faint rings circling it. Neptune has faint rings too, but only eight moons. One, Triton, is nearly as big as our Moon.

Ice world

After astronomers found Neptune, they carried on looking for new planets. But it was not until 1930 that they found another one. It was called Pluto. Pluto is the smallest planet. It is made up of rock and water ice. Its surface is covered with frozen gases. Gases freeze into solid ice when they get very cold. And Pluto is very cold indeed (-230°C).

Pluto has one moon, called Charon. Surprisingly, it is half the size of Pluto. And it always stays in the same spot in Pluto's sky. No other moons do this.

△ Half-size
Pluto and its moon Charon, which is half its size.

▽ Moonrise
Charon appears huge from the deep-frozen surface of Pluto.

Mini-planets

The planets formed millions of years ago when lumps of rock and other materials smashed into one another and stuck together. Some lumps were left over. We find many of them today circling the Sun between Mars and Jupiter. We call these lumps the asteroids.

△ Gaspra
18 km long

▷ Eros
24 km long

△ Ida
56 km long

Asteroid hit

There are thousands of asteroids. The largest is Ceres, about 1000 kilometres across. But most are much smaller. Most asteroids circle the Sun in a band, called the asteroid belt.

But some wander among the planets. A few sometimes stray near the Earth. Millions of years ago, asteroids may have hit the Earth. The dinosaurs might have been wiped out by an asteroid hit.

Probing the planets

Once we could only study the planets from afar with our eyes and through telescopes. But today we can study the planets close-up using spacecraft we call **probes**.

Space probes are launched by rocket or space shuttle and may take years to reach their target planet. They carry cameras and other instruments to record a planet's weather, for example.

Since the 1960s, space probes have explored all the planets except Pluto. The probe *Mariner 10* (1974) gave us our first pictures of Mercury, and *Magellan* (1990) revealed the great lava plains of Venus. *Cassini* will reach Saturn in 2004. But the most successful probe is *Voyager 2*. Launched in 1977, it visited Jupiter, Saturn, Uranus and Neptune.

Cassini drops the Huygens probe to land on Saturn's largest moon, Titan.

Useful words

asteroids Lumps of rock that circle the Sun between Mars and Jupiter.

atmosphere The layer of gases around a planet.

crater A hole in the surface of a planet or moon, made by a meteorite hitting it.

gas giant One of the four biggest planets, Jupiter, Saturn, Uranus or Neptune.

gravity The pull every lump of matter has on every other lump.

liquid gas A gas that has turned into liquid.

meteorite A lump of rock or metal from outer space.

moon A smaller body that circles around a planet.

phases of the Moon The changing shapes of the Moon during the month.

planet A large body that circles the Sun.

probe A spacecraft sent to explore distant planets.

ring A ring of particles circling round a planet.

Solar System The Sun's family, including the planets, their moons and comets.

volcano A mountain or hole in a planet's surface that pours out molten rock or other material.

Index